W9-CPC-095

DIVING AND SNORKELING GUIDE TO

Florida's East Coast

Including
Palm Beach
Ft. Lauderdale
and ## Miami areas

by Greg Johnston
and the editors of Pisces Books

Pisces Books • New York

Publishers Note: At the time of publication of this book, all the information was determined to be as accurate as possible. However, when you use this guide, new construction may have changed land reference points, weather may have altered reef configurations, and some businesses may no longer be functioning. Your assistance in keeping future editions up-to-date will be greatly appreciated. Also, please pay particular attention to the diver rating system in this book. Know your limits!

Copyright © 1987 by Pisces Book Co., Inc.
All rights reserved. No part of this book may be reproduced in any form whatsoever without written permission of the publisher. For information about this book write:
Pisces Book Co., Inc., One School Street, Glen Cove, NY 11542

Library of Congress Cataloging in Publication Data

Johnston, Greg.
Diving and snorkeling guide to Florida's East Coast.

Includes index.
1. Skin diving--Florida--Guide-books. 2. Scuba diving--Florida--Guide-books. 3. Florida--Description and travel--1981--Guide-books. I. Pisces Books (Firm) II. Title.
GV840.S78J64   1986   797.2'3'09759   86-30515
ISBN 0-86636-077-8

All photographs by the author except where otherwise noted.

Color separations by HongKong Scanner Craft Company Ltd., Hong Kong

Printed in Hong Kong

10   9   8   7   6   5   4   3   2   1

STAFF

Publisher	**Herb Taylor**
Project Director	**Cora Sibal Taylor**
Executive Editor	**Virginia Christensen**
Editor	**Joanne Bolnick**
Art Director	**Richard Liu**
Art/Prod. Coordinator	**Jeanette Forman**
Artist	**Daniel Kouw**

Table of Contents

How to Use This Guide

This underwater guide book provides the diver with the location, terrain, and many of the principle dive sites on Florida's east coast. It is important to note that while this book covers the most frequently visited sites, the environmental regulatory commissions of Dade, Broward and Palm Beach counties are continually adding new artificial reefs to the waters of South Florida.

The artificial reef sites have become very popular with both fishing and scuba charters. Many of the old derelict freighters used for building artificial reefs have been placed in deep water for the commercial and recreational sport fishermen, and many have been placed in shallower locations for divers.

Divers with proper training and open water experience should consider diving on the artificial reefs. Because many of the wrecks have been sunk in the 100-foot-depth range, and the prevalent current conditions vary with each location, it is wise to have proper training by a recognized certifying agency. Also, a working knowledge of the no-decompression tables is a good safeguard against any diving sickness or accident.

Seeing one of these majestic-looking wrecks for the first time is an exhilarating experience. It is urged that, whether you are a regular wreck diver or a first-time visitor, you practice conservation, courtesy and boating safety.

Turtles are common in areas off Palm Beach. In early summer, they deposit their eggs on the beach, and a few months later the tiny hatchlings race back to the water.

Divers with proper training and open water experience should consider diving on the artificial reefs. Because many of the wrecks have been sunk in the 100-foot depth range, and the prevalent current conditions vary with each location, it is wise to have proper training by a recognized certifying agency. ➤

The Rating System for Divers and Dives

The suggestions given in this guide for the minimum level of experience should be taken in a conservative sense. Each diver should know his or her level of experience and limitations. Remember the old rule: **Plan your dive and dive your plan.** For the purposes of this book, we consider a *novice* diver to be someone in good physical condition, who has only recently been certified, has not dived in the past twelve months or is unfamiliar with the waters. An *intermediate* level diver is someone in good physical condition who either has been actively diving in the past twelve months or is familiar with the waters. An *advanced* diver is someone in good physical condition who has achieved an advanced level of diving certification and regularly dives in similar waters. It is good advice to dive with someone who has more experience than you, or with the divemaster when on a professional charter.

Divers enjoy a leisurely swim over a ledge overgrown with sea life.

Divers in Palm Beach explore a reef for signs of life. Look closely for tiny marine organisms that sit in the crevices. Photograph by Steven Lucas

1

Overview of Florida's East Coast

The Calusa Indians were the first inhabitants of Florida's east coast. The Indians occupied much of the Florida Keys and areas along the banks of the Miami River, which is now part of downtown Miami. The first European known to have explored the Florida coast was the Spanish navigator Juan Ponce de Leon. Then the governor of Puerto Rico, Ponce de Leon led an expedition westward to search for an island believed to be the site of the "fountain of Youth."

Ponce de Leon first landed near the present city of Jacksonville in March of 1513. Inspired by the rich vegetation, Ponce de Leon called the new land "Florida" (Spanish for flowery), and sailed south along the coast. Ponce de Leon never did find the fountain of youth, but the Spanish explorer was determined to colonize the new land. The following year he returned to Spain to ask for royal sanction and support.

During the next 40 years, the Spanish returned to Florida and explored the land extensively in an attempt to colonize it. However, each new Spanish settlement continued to be harassed and discouraged by the natives.

France soon attempted to colonize Florida in 1534. King Philip II of Spain, fearing he would lose claims to the land, dispatched an expedition to capture the French colonies and return the land to Spain.

Britain tried several unsuccessful attempts to drive the Spanish from Florida, and finally, in 1763 Spain ceded the land to Britain for the return of Havana.

The second Spanish occupation came in 1783 when, after the American Revolution, Britain returned Florida to Spain in return for the Bahama Islands. This was a period of constant friction between the Spanish authorities and the American settlers. Weakened by the declining economy in Europe, Spain was unable to maintain order in the new land and, in 1819, sold Florida to the young United States. Florida joined the union and became a state in 1845.

After 1876 Florida underwent a process of change and development that continued into the twentieth century. The population increased, and with the great influx of people, new cities were built and railroad transportation was extended from Jacksonville to the Keys. Florida became a center for agricultural, mineral and industrial production. Tourism flourished as Florida's greatest industry.

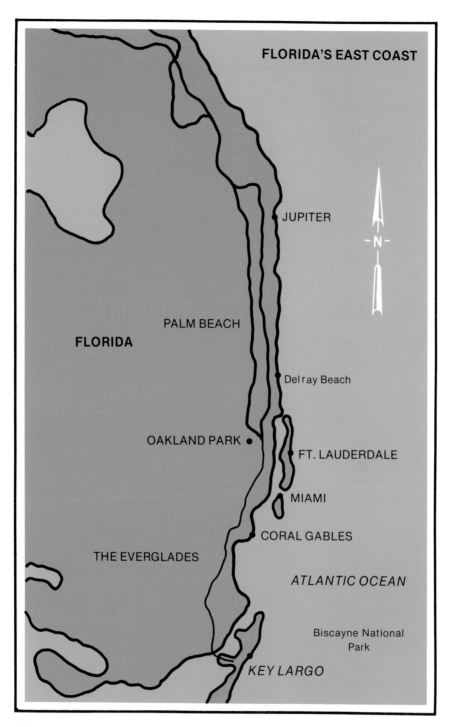

The eastern coast of Florida, an area rich in history, attracts numerous tourists. Much of Florida's success in tourism is attributable to the exceptional diving and snorkeling in the clear blue waters of the Atlantic.

The East Coast Today

Miami. Miami has grown over the past 20 years. Once a small tourist community, where only the rich and famous vacationed, Miami has prospered into a city of commerce and the hub to all Caribbean travel. Miami International Airport is one of the busiest airports in the country, servicing both international and domestic flights daily. The Port of Miami is home to the largest fleet of cruise ships in the world. Over a dozen cruise ships leave the seaport weekly, taking passengers on high-sea adventures to ports of call in the Caribbean islands.

Miami is home to the annual International Grand Prix race, where many of the top competitive drivers in the world compete through the downtown streets. It is also the location of the annual football classic in the Orange Bowl, and the nationally televised King Orange Parade. Miami is a very diverse and cultural city with many fine restaurants, night clubs and entertaining attractions.

Ft. Lauderdale. Since the release of the movie "Where The Boys Are," Ft. Lauderdale has been considered a beach town. Each year during the college spring break, the Lauderdale strip becomes crowded with students. Ft. Lauderdale has many fine restaurants, night clubs and discos, but the beach remains the biggest attraction.

Port Everglades, the city harbor and one of the deepest ports on the east coast of the U.S., serves the region's vegetable, citrus fruit and other fruit industries. A leading industry in this resort city, itself, is fishing. Ft. Lauderdale is the sight of many national fishing tournaments and home to one of the largest charter fishing fleets in Florida.

West Palm Beach. Palm Beach remains the noted and fashionable winter home to the very rich and famous. A drive down Highway A1A is a sight to behold. The road is lined with sprawling mansions and rolling sand dunes. It is a place for surfing and sunbathing, expensive cars and chic restaurants. The town has facilities for fishing and boating, including a yacht basin at Lake Worth and an extensive public beach.

Christmas tree worms dot the reefs of Florida. Photographers will get some good close-up shots if they approach quietly. These little organisms retreat quickly when warned.

Weather Patterns

Summer. During the summer months, diving is at its best. Weather conditions are usually predictable, although the summer months do tend to have late afternoon thunderstorms. Water and air temperature conditions are near perfect. The seas are usually flat and calm and tip the Fahrenheit scale at 85 degrees, while the air temperatures range in the high 80s to the low 90s. Summertime not only is the season for waterspouts, but also for tropical storms, low atmospheric depressions and hurricanes. It is best to check with local weather authorities before venturing out for the day.

Winter. Boating activities do continue during the winter months, but with less frequency. Winter marks the season of cold fronts moving in from the north, and much rougher sea conditions. The water temperatures drop to about 72 degrees, and the air temperatures range in the mid 70s. Typically, the winter winds blow from the northeast, against the Gulf Stream, causing seas that can exceed five feet.

11

Water Conditions

Those who dive regularly off southeast Florida have at one time or another experienced strong currents. The Gulf Stream hugs the Florida coastline very closely and the currents vary depending on tidal changes and distance from shore. Since beach diving is more popular in the Ft. Lauderdale and Palm Beach areas, it is important to note the types of currents and how to handle yourself should you be caught.

Longshore Currents. These are the strong currents that flow in a northern path. If caught in this type of current it is best to inflate your buoyancy compensator, notify the boat captain of your intentions, drift with the current, and kick slowly towards the beach if it is not a long distance away. If you are on a charter, the dive captain will eventually pick you up after all the other divers are on board.

Backwash. These currents go only a short distance offshore and do not normally tow anyone under. The most danger from this type of current is the possibility of knocking a diver off balance and the loss of diving equipment.

Rip Currents. Rip currents occur when a large volume of water is forced through a narrow opening such as a sandbar. Do not try to fight this type of current, but swim at right angles to the current and eventually back to shore.

Other Currents. Offshore, other currents occur because of a variety of factors, including eddies, tides, wind and bottom contours that create ground swells. Such currents may vary in direction and speed. When diving from the beach it is always good practice to check current conditions. If the current is very strong, terminate the dive.

A hungry green moray looks eye-to-eye with a diver at Jupiter High Ledge. Most morays used to divers are quite friendly. Photograph by Steven Lucas ➤

The Natural Reefs

The natural reefs of southeast Florida extend from the Dry Tortugas near Key West north to Jupiter in Palm Beach county. The reefs do extend further north than Jupiter, but are generally in much deeper water and not as well developed. The coral reefs south of Miami are typical of the reefs found throughout the Florida Keys. The coral reef system discussed in this guide are found offshore between Miami and Jupiter. These coral reefs are considered atypical because the ledges have few tropical corals.

This tract of coral reef has been growing since the Pleistocene period, about 95,000 years ago. At one time in history, these reefs were similar to the reefs found today in the Florida Keys. Today, the reefs consist mostly of hard corals, such as star corals, starlet corals and brain corals.

There are three reef lines. The first begins close to the shore in less than 12 feet of water and is about 200 feet wide. The reef is a low profile coral, with ledges not more than one to two feet high. The reef starts just below the tide mark and is largely covered by sand.

Between the first and second reef line, the ocean floor is a sloping barren sand flat. The second reef line is a representation of small coral patches located about 500 yards from shore. The width of the reef varies, but it is usually around 300 feet wide. Depths range in the 25- to 40-foot mark.

The third reef line is over 1-1/2 miles offshore in 70 to 100 feet of water and is the most popular reef line among divers. This coral reef has well-developed corals and an abundance of marine life. The coral ridges rise more than 10 feet from the sand floor and are flushed continuously by the warm currents of the Gulf Stream.

Artificial Reefs

Florida's southeast coast has quickly become the shipwreck capital of the world—and for good reasons. Since 1981, the Dade County Artificial Reef Program has been sinking old derelict freighters, concrete culvert pipes, construction rubble, and large metal objects off Miami's coastline. As a result of the favorable response to the Dade County program, Broward and Palm Beach county environmental resources departments have also begun a very successful artificial reef program. The artificial reefs enhance the fish population and bring new excitement to recreational sport diving.

Artificial reefs are not a new idea. They have existed for over 200 years. The Japanese were the first to use artificial reefs, primarily to expand the commercial fishing industry.

New artificial reefs can be created by placing man-made objects in barren areas of the ocean floor. When these materials are placed in depths where sunlight penetrates, photosynthesis occurs. The objects quickly become colonized with miniature marine organisms. The algae and corals begin to attract other creatures such as crabs, lobsters, and schools of bait fish. This rich food source, in turn, attracts many of the ocean's larger predatory fish, and soon the reef cycle begins.

This type of diverse and rich marine ecosystem is similar to a natural coral reef system in the way it works. In a relatively short period of time, what was once a flat, sand ocean bottom has been transformed into a thriving marine community.

All materials selected to be placed underwater are inspected carefully by the United States Coast Guard. These inspections are to insure that all pollutants are removed and that all loose hatches, debris and doors are removed from the vessels prior to sinking. The location for the sinking is carefully selected, and the ship is towed to its final resting place. The sinking is quickly performed, utilizing the expertise of the local police bomb squad. Several hundred tons of dynamite is placed strategically throughout the ship to insure quick, upright sinking.

Months of planning precedes the placing of material, which takes minutes to sink and only a few days to begin a new life as an artificial reef.

A large, colorful sea fan stands strong in the currents off Ft. Lauderdale. ➤

Dive Boats

Since most of the dive sites are not marked, it usually takes the keen eye of a charter boat captain to line up the shore landmarks. Unless divers are very familiar with the surrounding area, it is probably best to leave the navigating to one of the many professional charter boat operators.

The dive shops along the east coast are full-service stores with air fills, equipment rentals, sales and instruction. Many of the shops have their own dive boats that can accommodate a group of 20 divers or more.

The primary diving along the east coast is usually deep, and not very suitable for snorkelers. However, there are some very pretty shallow reefs near shore, and these sites are usually visited as a second dive. Some of these reefs are accessible from shore, and are very suitable for snorkelers.

All the east coast dive boats are Coast Guard certified and have at least one licensed captain and one experienced divemaster who is familiar with the area. Be sure to check for package deals and group rates.

The Florida wrecks are accessible by professional dive charter boats. Captains and experienced dive masters can assist divers and snorkelers in finding these sites and diving them safely. Dive shops along the east coast are full-service shops, and many have their own dive boats that can accommodate large groups of divers.

Fish and Game Regulations

You should be aware of these important Florida diving laws established by the Division of Fish and Game concerning various types of marine life.

Lobster. The lobster season opens on July 26 and ends on March 31. The special two-day diver's season is open July 20 and 21 (limit is 6 per day or 12 for both days). The lobster carapace must measure at least 3 inches and the tail not less than 5-1/2 inches. It is illegal to take egg-bearing females, or to remove the tail while at sea. The legal limit per person is 24, or 24 total per boat. It is unlawful to spear lobster, and a permit is required for trapping.

Stone Crab. Stone crab season opens on October 15 and ends on May 15. The stone crab claw must measure at least 2-3/4 inches. It is illegal to remove more than one claw from the crab.

Spearfishing. It is unlawful to spearfish near public beaches, fishing piers, jetties or bridges. It is also illegal to spear game fish or to spear in areas designated as marine sanctuaries.

Coral. It is unlawful to collect or possess any form of live coral, soft coral or sea fans. Most Florida dive operators have an unwritten law that will not allow any coral souvenirs on the dive boats.

Conch. It is illegal to take Queen conch in Florida waters.

Dive Flag Law. It is required while diving or snorkeling in state waters to provide a float and "divers-down" flag. A divers-down flag shall consist of a red background with a diagonal white stripe. Boaters are required to observe the flag and remain at a minimum distance of 100 yards.

"Divers-Down" Flag

Alpha Flag International signal meaning "I have a diver down; keep clear and at a slow speed"

2

Diving in Miami

Miami is one of those cities most traveling divers pass through on their way to destinations in the Caribbean or the Florida Keys. What these travelers don't realize is that they're missing the true beauty of wreck and reef diving in the Atlantic Ocean.

Miami offers top-notch dive shops and underwater tour guides. Diving in Miami is a year-round activity enjoyed by all watersport enthusiasts. The Dade County Artificial Reef Program has placed over two dozen abandoned freighters and old work boats, as well as a mixture of other debris, on the ocean floor—all within a 30-minute boat ride of each other.

Most dive sites are only accessible by boat, and you will have to know the locations of the dive sites to find them. All the dive locations are marked by Loran readings, compass bearings or shore targets. Reef and wreck locations can be obtained from any professional shop in Miami. There is very little shore diving in Miami. Unlike Ft. Lauderdale and Palm Beach, the Gulf Stream is much farther from shore. But, if you choose to operate your own boat or rent one, there are numerous boat rental companies and public marinas.

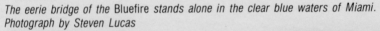

The eerie bridge of the Bluefire *stands alone in the clear blue waters of Miami. Photograph by Steven Lucas*

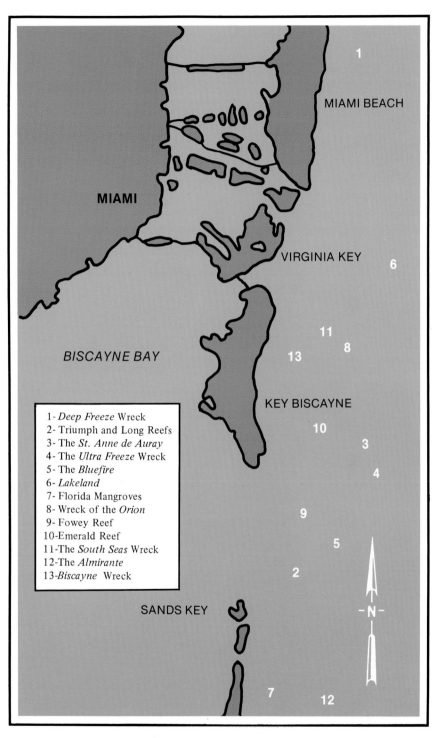

The waters off Miami offer exceptional diving experiences. Divers often are unaware of the many wrecks and colorful reefs accessible by a short boat ride.

Deep Freeze Wreck   1

Typical depth range	:	135 feet
Typical current conditions	:	Variable, medium
Expertise required	:	Intermediate to advanced
Access	:	Boat

The Deep Freeze is one of the deeper Miami wrecks but is not considered a hard wreck to dive. The 210-foot freighter now rests intact at a maximum depth of 135 feet with over 25 feet of relief. Most of the superstructure was removed prior to its sinking in October of 1976; however, the deck and some of the cabins remain. This wreck is easily located. It lies north of

Marine organisms have made the Deep Freeze *their permanent home. Photograph by Steven Lucas*

The Deep Freeze *lies in about 135 feet of water. Watch your bottom time and depth carefully. Photograph by Steven Lucas*

Government Cut at the mouth of the main port channel, close to the Miami Beach shoreline.

What makes this wreck incredible are the colonies of spiny oysters. The oyster family, which is part of the mollusk group, has over fifty living species and most are edible. The shell of the spiny oyster is irregularly oval in shape. It consists of a left and right valve joined by an elastic ligament which acts as a hinge. The inner surfaces are like smooth porcelain, and the outer shell has pointy spines from which it derives its name. No seasonal limit applies to the taking of oysters. Usually the depth of the Deep Freeze will dictate the amount of oysters one will pry from the wreck.

There is always an abundance of bait fish around the bow of the vessel, and with the life-supporting food fish, there is always the chance to see some of the larger ocean predators. The Deep Freeze is an exciting wreck for the visiting or the seasoned Miami diver.

Typical depth range	:	20-80 feet
Typical current conditions	:	None to slight
Expertise required	:	Novice
Access	:	Boat

Biscayne Bay and the natural patch reefs that extend from Key Biscayne in Miami to the northern tip of Key Largo form the boundaries of Biscayne National Monument Park. Within the park are several reefs that offer types of coral and marine life similar to those found in the reefs of the keys. Triumph Reef and Long Reef are two of the healthiest and popular in the Miami area.

Triumph Reef is located south of Sands Cut, the inlet between Elliott Key and Sand Key. This reef is a spur and groove coral formation with many winding sand paths and high profile star and pillar corals. There are several undercuts and ledges, and coral formations that resemble caves. Each coral penetration allows the diver to swim from one side of the reef to the other. Often large oceanic pelagic creatures frequent this area, largely because of the proximity of the Gulf Stream. Large manta rays have been reported seen at this reef, as well as sea turtles and an occasional shark.

Long Reef is an excellent site for repetitive diving, underwater photography and night diving. Seaward of the buoy that marks the shallow reef is a

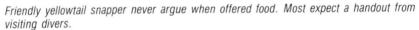

Friendly yellowtail snapper never argue when offered food. Most expect a handout from visiting divers.

Divers at Triumph and Long Reef will enjoy the ledges and coral formations. This is an excellent spot for photography.

steeply sloping ledge that extends from a depth of 45 feet to over 80 feet before levelling out to a flat sandy bottom. Large basket sponges cover the entire reef and whispy sea whips flow in the gentle currents. There are rows of staghorn corals and patches of elkhorn coral. A carpet of lavender sea fans crests the top of the reef, and parrot fish are often found dining on the coral and shells. There is a deeper reef at 100 feet, but the current is sometimes strong, and unless planned as a drift dive, not recommended. It is best to stay closer to the shallower reef.

For the very experienced diver there are two deep coral heads in 120 feet of water situated almost exactly between Triumph Reef and Long Reef. The current is usually very strong; however, when the tides are slack, it is easy to find these coral mounds and dive them. Rising more than 20 feet from the sandy bottom, and measuring over 15 feet in diameter, each mound is a world unto itself. As in all deep dives, bottom time is very limited.

Be cautious—deep diving can be life-threatening. You should be careful not to exceed the safe no-decompression limits and dive with someone of equal or greater experience.

Typical depth range	:	70 feet
Typical current conditions	:	Variable to strong
Expertise required	:	Novice to intermediate
Access	:	Boat

The St. Anne de Auray, commonly called the Auray by local Miami charters, is one of the most recent ships purposely sunk by Dade County to create an artificial reef. The 110-foot trawler was sunk in 70 feet of water off the southern tip of Key Biscayne in March of 1986.

This ship is completely intact and sits upright with a slight list to the starboard side. The superstructure remains intact offering over 28 feet of

The St. Anne de Auray was recently sunk as an artificial reef in Miami. Here a diver passes by an air vent of the 100-foot trawler.

There are many interesting parts of the St. Anne de Auray *left to explore. The ship is still intact in 70 feet of water.*

relief. This wreck makes an excellent location for novice wreck divers because of the relatively shallow water and the short length of the hull. There is not much to see off the ship—the best is around the ship's capstan, air vents and upper bridge. The engine room is accessible but thick silt and grease make it undesirable. Inside the main salon of the ship is a school of copper sweepers that part in unison as you swim through.

The cargo holds are easily accessible and offer the exploring diver an opportunity to see the hull of the ship. The sunken vessel is an excellent photo prop. It would not take much of an imagination to come up with some very exciting photographs after a dive on this wreck.

The Auray is easily found by using the visual range of one finger's distance at arms length, between Cape Florida Light on the south end of Key Biscayne and the tower of the Biltmore Hotel in downtown Coral Gables.

This is a good wreck for extended bottom time, but be sure to check current conditions. When the Gulf Stream moves close to shore the currents can exceed 3 knots, far stronger than even the best swimmer can handle.

Typical depth range	:	120 feet
Typical current conditions	:	Variable to strong
Expertise required	:	Intermediate
Access	:	Boat

When several hundred tons of dynamite thundered through her hull, the proud ship Ultra Freeze shuddered slightly, and with a slow sluggish roll the ship slipped beneath the waves in less than one minute.

The Ultra Freeze was sunk in July of 1984 after being docked in the Miami River for a long period of inactive sea duty. The 195-foot steel freighter, like the wrecked Deep Freeze, was a former refrigerator ship that carried cargos of beef, vegetables and other items.

The South Florida Spearfishing Council is mostly responsible for the sinking of the Ultra Freeze. The club sponsored many fund raising activities to clean the ship and remove all entrapping objects, like doors, from the vessel prior to sinking. The vessel was towed to a sight about two miles north of Fowey Reef Lighthouse near the southern tip of Key Biscayne, where it was sunk.

The ship today has attracted a large colony of marine creatures that have now made their home among the cargo holds and decks of the vessel. The ship rests in 120 feet of water with over 50 feet of relief. Diving the upper deck and cabins, which are at a depth of 70 feet is good for the novice or the diver who wants to get back into diving after a period of landlubbing.

A flashlight comes in quite handy when observing parts of a wreck. This diver is next to the propeller of the Ultra Freeze.

A diver peers through the cargo hatch of the sunken freighter, Ultra Freeze.

Typical depth range	:	110 feet
Typical current conditions	:	Variable to strong
Expertise required	:	Intermediate
Access	:	Boat

The Bluefire is one of the few Miami wrecks that cannot easily be described. It has to be dived to fully appreciate its true beauty as a shipwreck. The 175-foot steel vessel is a former island cargo freighter that was based in Key West. The ship made frequent calls to ports in the Caribbean until its final calling in the spring of 1980 when several hundred thousand Cuban citizens arrived at Key West during the Mariel boatlift. The Bluefire took part in the historical exodus, and it was seized by the U.S. Department of Immigration and Naturalization.

The Bluefire sat vacant in a Miami boatyard for almost two years before authorities decided what to do with the ship. In January of 1983 the

A diver hovers above the ghostly ladder leading to the bridge of the Bluefire wreck.

The Bluefire *truly conjures up memories for those who dive Florida's waters. It was used for the Mariel boatlift in 1980.*

ship was donated to the Dade County Artificial Reef Program and sunk in 110 feet of water.

The ship can be located off the southern edge of Soldiers Key in Biscayne Bay. Align the towers of the Cutler Ridge Florida Power and Light smoke stacks one finger's distance from the southern edge of Soldiers Key. Set the depth finder on your boat for 110 feet, and you should be right over the wreck.

The wreck today is an underwater photographer's dream. The fully intact Bluefire sits upright with over 30 feet of relief. The classic wreck looks the way you would imagine a shipwreck to look, a ghostly remnant from the past. The deck gear, winches and radar mast are still intact, making excellent photo props. The main bridge and cabins are accessible and portholes still line the corridors. This wreck is a natural fish haven. Huge numbers of hogfish and jacks cruise the gangways while small tropical fish flutter among the ladders and hatches. If you dive in Miami, do not miss this wreck!

Typical depth range	:	120-140 feet
Typical current conditions	:	Strong
Expertise required	:	Advanced
Access	:	Boat

The 200-foot steel freighter was purposely sunk in June of 1982 to serve as part of the Dade County Artificial Reef Program. The Lakeland has two sister wrecks, the Arida and the Shamrock, all former landing craft utility (LCU) vessels. The Lakeland was reportedly used during the U.S. military action in Vietnam, and then later sold for non-military, commercial use.

The Lakeland is a flat-bottomed vessel with two large propellers at the stern. The vessel is lying on its side in 126 to 140 feet of water. This is one of

A landing craft utility vessel used by the U.S. military, the Lakeland, *was purposely sunk in about 120 feet of water. It is now home to numerous fish and corals.*

A diver explores the wheelhouse of the Lakeland.

the deeper wreck dives that is visited on a regular basis. The Arida is on its side and the Shamrock is upside down. The LCUs, probably because of their flat bottom and top-heavy structures, never settle right side up when they sink.

Today, the wreck of the Lakeland is one of the most exciting dive sites. The ship has attracted large numbers of schooling fish like bait fish and grunts. The wreck has numerous openings and hatches that make secret hiding places for the tropical fish that homestead on the Lakeland's deck. Fish that know the maze of a wreck are generally much safer from predators that lurk outside the wreck. Schooling bait fish protect themselves by remaining in tight formation. The larger predatory fish usually will feed on stragglers and lone fish.

The wreck is easily located outside the main port channel in downtown Miami. Align the red-and-white checkered water tower of Virginia Key with the north edge of One Biscayne Tower in downtown Miami. The visual mark should put you on top of the wreck in 140 feet of water.

Typical depth range	:	5-10 feet
Typical current conditions	:	Variable, sometimes very strong
Expertise required	:	None
Access	:	Boat or beach

Biscayne Bay is located south of Miami and consists of over 180,000 square acres of patch reefs, seagrass beds and sub-tropical islands. The pristine waters of the bay extend south from Key Biscayne to John Pennekamp Park in Key Largo. From the curve of the 10-fathom line the bay flows westward to the mangrove-covered shores of south Dade County.

For the visiting diver, a look into the web of mangrove roots will reveal a wealth of undersea life. For the underwater photographer the mangroves are a macro world of blood red sponges, clusters of orange-tipped tunicates and small blue crabs. Often schools of grunts and snapper can be found

Marine life is abundant in the shallow waters near the mangroves of Biscayne Bay.

here as well as large rays and an occasional shark. It is not uncommon to find the lovable sea mammal, the manatee, carelessly munching on a snack of mangrove roots and leaves.

The mangroves are easily accessible from shore or from boat. They are bathed daily in fresh, warm, clear ocean water. Many channels cut through the leafy forests and create ledges beneath the waterline. Damaging wakes from passing motorboats have eroded the underlying substrate, creating intricate cave-like tunnels.

Photography in the mangroves can be exciting and creative. Because the water is usually very still, interesting reflections from the mirrored surface create unusual effects.

Be careful not to kick up silt, as visibility can be quickly reduced to nearly zero. Try to move slowly, use a gentle flutter kick when possible, or pull yourself along through the roots by your hands. Caution is advised during tidal changes because the current can be very strong and can pull you away from the safety of your boat.

This aerial photograph shows one of the mangrove-covered islands of Florida.

Typical depth range	:	95 feet
Typical current conditions	:	Variable; intermediate to strong
Expertise required	:	Intermediate
Access	:	Boat

The Orion is one of those classic-looking shipwrecks, perhaps like something out of your imagination. Descending the anchor line from the dive boat above, the first impression new divers have of the Orion is of a silhouetted ghost ship underway along the bottom of the Atlantic Ocean.

The Orion was sunk in December of 1981, after being declared a derelict vessel and removed from the Miami River. It is a 120-foot ocean-going tugboat sitting intact with a slight list to the starboard side 95 feet below the surface.

The 120-foot tugboat Orion *was sunk in 1981. Today it hosts a variety of colorful sea life, and it is a popular dive spot off Miami.*

Recommended for the intermediate diver, the wreck of the Orion *is a spectacular, memorable wreck dive.*

The history of the ship is not quite clear. It was reportedly used during the widening of the Panama Canal. Today, the superstructure of the wreck is intact, inviting the visiting diver to explore the pilot house, engine rooms and the cabins below.

The Orion is alive with color. Many small macro marine organisms now cover the entire tugboat, and long, soft corals flow gently in the currents. For the underwater photographer, the Orion is a perfect backdrop for exciting photographs.

One of the most photogenic sections of the wreck is the large propeller. The hub of the wheel is at 95 feet, allowing the diver only 25 safe no-decompression minutes at this depth. The wreck has about 30 feet of relief, and if you choose to remain on the upper deck you can increase your bottom time. However, choose your bottom time carefully—twenty minutes on this wreck is enough time to get a taste of Miami wreck diving.

Typical depth range	:	30-50 feet
Typical current conditions	:	Mild
Expertise required	:	Novice
Access	:	Boat

Fowey Reef Light, one of the many iron-piled lighthouses located within the sweeping chain of reefs along the Florida Keys, marks the location of Fowey Reef. The 165-foot steel lighthouse tower, which can be seen up to 12 miles off the Florida coast, was built over 100 years ago by Lt. George Meade, who served in the Civil War.

Fowey Reef is not without its share of historic shipwrecks. Recently, a mysterious wreck was discovered by a local diver. The wreck revealed a solid brass ship's bell from an early-dated British man-of-war.

Divers of all abilities will find Fowey Reef an enjoyable dive. This diver is welcomed by a school of grunts.

Located in the Florida Keys, the Fowey Reef lighthouse is a 100-year-old marker for the historic Fowey Reef off Miami.

Today, Fowey Reef is alive and healthy. Unlike the populated reefs of the Keys, Fowey is seldom visited. Visibility generally exceeds 70 feet, and on a warm summer day, only a handful of pleasure craft displaying the diver's flag can be found anchored here.

The reef offers a steep sloping dropoff that starts in 40 feet of water, just east of the lighthouse, and sharply tapers to over 90 feet before levelling off to a soft, sandy bottom.

The reef is a spur and groove system, with long winding sand chutes that twist through coral fissures. South of the light are massive stands of elkhorn corals that rise to within a few feet of the surface. On the west side of the light are forests of staghorn corals, and to the west and south are mountainous star and cavernous starlet corals.

This is a good reef system for novice through advanced divers. The easy access and no apparent currents make Fowey Reef one of the more popular reef sites for local divers.

Typical depth range	:	10-30 feet
Typical current conditions	:	None
Expertise required	:	Novice
Access	:	Boat

Emerald Reef is one of the more popular middle reef sites located a few miles east of Key Biscayne. A small reef, it is situated among sections of the overall reef line that makes up the Miami reefs.

The middle reef, found off Miami, supports a well-defined coral reef system. Similar in many ways to the reefs in the Florida Keys, Emerald Reef has elkhorn and pillar corals, as well as an assortment of hard and soft corals. The fish population is abundant, and a wandering green moray eel that measures about six feet long is often seen here.

Common to this reef are the deep purple sea fans, some precariously perched on top of large coral heads. These sea fans flow gently in the light surge and are anchored by a vibrant purple-hued stem. Often the lacy sea fan is used by macro photographers as a backdrop for the very photogenic flamingo tongue shell, which is commonly found grazing on the algae trapped in the sea fans' filigree network.

The flamingo tongue shell is about an inch long and has an oval flesh-colored shell. The mantle, or skin, emerges as a transparent yellow with golden leopard spots outlined in black over the highly polished shell.

Emerald Reef's large coral reef system hosts various coral assortments.

Miami offers fantastic diving for the visiting or native diver. The Artificial Reef Program has shown excellent results.

Typical depth range	:	70 feet
Typical current conditions	:	Variable, mild
Expertise required	:	Novice
Access	:	Boat

The wreck of the South Seas is one of the more infamous artificial reefs found off Miami. The 150-foot luxury yacht was built in 1928 for the well-known industrial family, Guggenheim. The ship was built to the exact specifications of its sister ship, which was Adolf Hitler's private yacht. The yacht South Seas changed hands through the years and was owned by several wealthy families, including the Woolworth family.

By the early 1980s, the ship had served its purpose well. Many important people had walked the decks, and the ship showed signs of deteriora-

A French angelfish poses for a photographer around the South Seas *wreck, an artificial reef.*

Colorful starfish provide the foreground for this picture of the South Seas *wreck.*
Photograph by Steven Lucas

tion. Private investors purchased the ship attempting to restore the proud vessel. The South Seas sat in a canal in Miami for several years, where it sank more than once. The luxury yacht was finally considered too old for expensive repairs and was donated to the county's artificial reef program.

Problems occurred while the South Seas was being towed to its final resting place. It sank twice while under tow. Finally in February of 1983 the ship was sunk a few miles east of downtown Miami in 70 feet of water.

Today, much of the ship's wooden structure has collapsed. The hull sits upright with the bow pointing towards the surface. The wreck is shrouded in bait fish, marine tropicals and dozens of Queen angelfish. An ominous-looking school of barracuda seems to hang just above the wreck. Although they seem well-fed, it is still unnerving to swim through these curious fish to get to the wreck.

This is a good wreck dive for the newly certified diver and is generally used as a night dive location or for scuba classes.

The ship was the setting for a live underwater TV broadcast during a local Miami news program. It is believed to be the first such live telecast of its kind for a TV news show.

Typical depth range	:	122-132 feet
Typical current conditions	:	Very strong
Expertise required	:	Experienced
Access	:	Boat

The Almirante was a U.S. Army supply ship during the second world war. Most of the action the ship saw was during the U.S. occupation of the South Pacific. After the war, the ship was sold and used for the transport of cargo through the Caribbean. The years had taken their toll on the once proud ship, and soon the Almirante was retired in a Miami shipyard. In April of 1975, the Almirante was declared a derelict freighter and towed to a final resting place 130 feet below the surface.

Coral grows along the wreck of the Almirante.

Covered in a variety of hard and soft corals, the Almirante *wreck is a popular dive spot for the experienced wreck diver. Currents can be very strong.*

Today, the 200-foot-long Almirante sits a few miles off the northern tip of Elliot Key. The vessel is upright, though all of the superstructure has been removed, and the wood decking has given way.

Because of the extreme current conditions that usually exist and the depth involved, only experienced divers should attempt to dive this wreck. Fortunately, this wreck is hard to find because of the lack of shore coordinates. However, Loran coordinates are available, but it is still wise to dive with only professional operators and divers who are familiar with the sea conditions.

The Almirante is the most colorful of all the Miami wrecks. The structure is covered in soft and hard corals. Deep water gorgonian align her ribs, reminiscent of the South Pacific flora. Large oceanic animals constantly cruise the wreck, and many deep water fish call this vessel home.

There is not much to see in the areas surrounding the structure, and divers are urged to remain on the deck and take careful notice of their bottom time and limitations.

Typical depth range	:	55 feet
Typical current conditions	:	Variable, mild
Expertise required	:	Novice
Access	:	Boat

The actual name of this wreck has been obscured, but the present name stands for the wreck's location, Key Biscayne. This wreck was one of the first wrecks dived in the Miami area. It has been sunken for more than 14 years and is still the most popular of the east coast wrecks. The 120-foot island freighter sits nearly intact in less than 60 feet of water on a flat sandy bottom, an easy setting for divers. It is an excellent place for new divers, or for divers returning to the sea after an absence, to get a taste of Miami wreck diving.

The freighter carried a cargo of bananas between the islands until it was confiscated for financial reasons and sold to a group of commercial fishermen. The fishermen had the idea of towing the ship out to sea late one night and sinking it in a secret spot to create their own artificial reef. The hatches were pulled and the ship began to sink slowly, much slower than the

A gray angelfish accepts a morsel from a visiting diver.

Framed inside an opening in the Biscayne *wreck, a diver searches for good photo opportunities.* ➤

The Biscayne *wreck, named after its location in Florida, is a 120-foot freighter. Look carefully for its many friendly inhabitants.*

fishermen anticipated. A December storm was brewing and the winds and waves began to drift the ship closer to shore. The vessel finally came to rest in 55 to 60 feet of water, much to the dismay of the fishermen. Their plan to sink the ship in deeper water was fouled, and now the wreck was accessible to divers.

The wreck has many friendly inhabitants. Towards the stern of the ship, on the port side, is the coral-encrusted home of a small spotted moray eel. There are several other friendly eels on this wreck, and all have been hand-fed by local dive guides. Small food bits can entice these little creatures out of their homes to pose for photos.

Another treat for divers while exploring the Biscayne wreck is the large cargo holds that can be easily penetrated. Inside you will find swarms of bait fish and tropical reef fish.

Night diving on the wreck is a Miami favorite. All the nocturnal inhabitants come alive, while the daytime citizens retreat for safe hibernation. The deck is literally covered with scorpionfish, and divers must be aware of the infectious sting of the poisonous spines found along their dorsal fins.

This wreck can be easily located by aligning the striped stacks on Virginia Key with the northern edge of the Biscayne Tower building in downtown Miami. Set your depth finder to 55 feet and you should cross over the top of the wreck. On days when the surface chop is light, you can see the outline of the wreck below.

A spotted moray claims his right to the Biscayne *wreck.*

3

Diving in Ft. Lauderdale

Diving in Ft. Lauderdale has become increasingly popular, largely because of the famed wreck of the Mercedes. However, local divers knew the potential of the diving in Ft. Lauderdale for many years before the wreck existed. The clear waters of the Atlantic Ocean are constantly being cleansed by the warm currents of the Gulf Stream. With the currents come the life-supporting nutrients required for the healthy reef system to thrive.

The Ft. Lauderdale reefs consist of three separate coral ledges that run parallel to the beach. The inner reef is the closest to the beach and well within snorkeling distance. The middle reef is further out in 30 to 40 feet of water and is usually a good shallow dive. The outer reef is over a mile off-shore, with depths in the 60- to 80-foot range.

In addition to the many coral ledges found off Ft. Lauderdale, the Broward County Environmental Agency and the Broward County Diving Association have been sinking derelict freighters and other discarded objects outside the outer reef line creating fish havens for visiting divers. The artificial reef program has been very successful, and new wrecks are continually being added to the already popular wrecks listed in this book.

A large spiny lobster peeks out of its rocky home at Lobster Ledge.

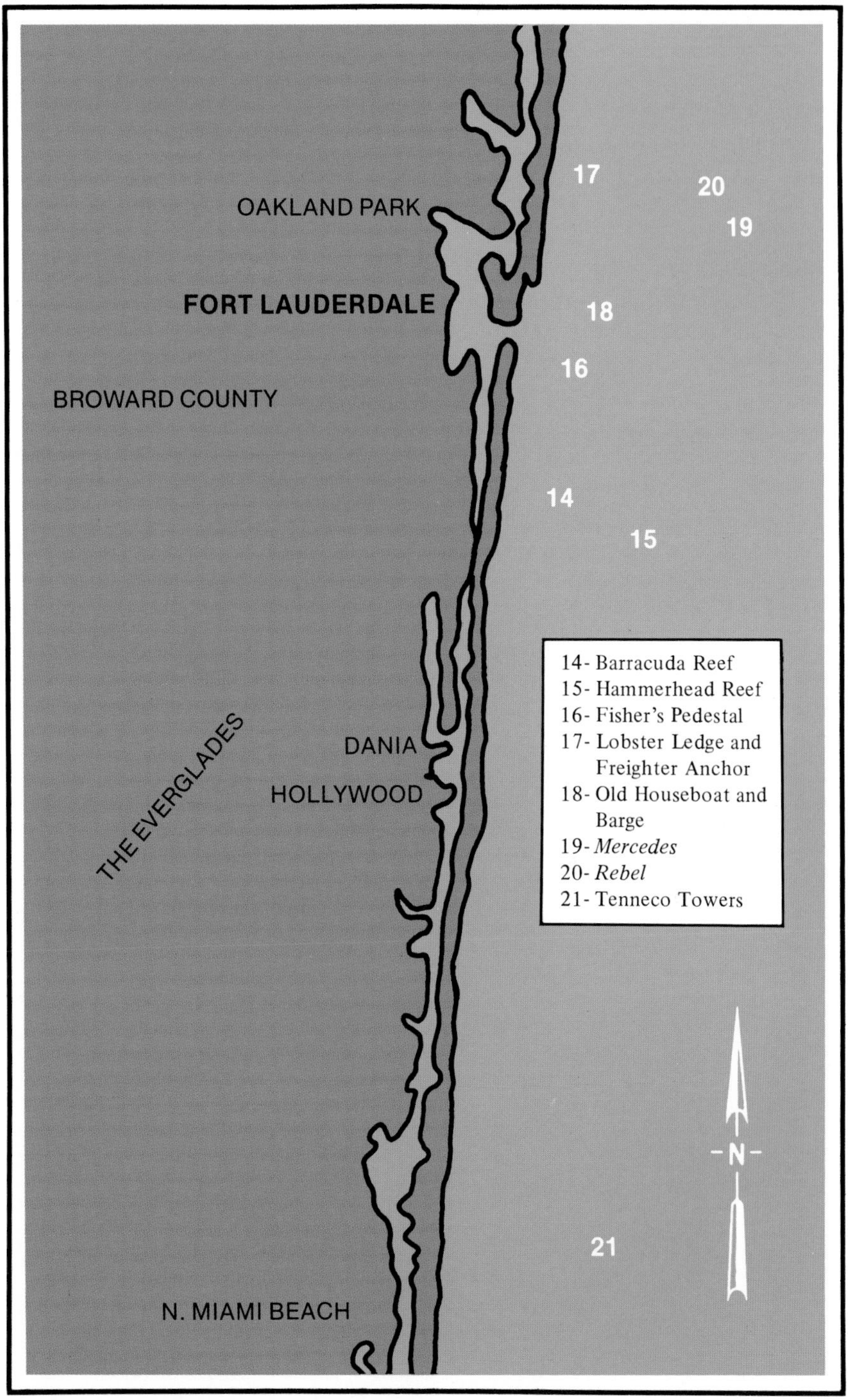
OAKLAND PARK
FORT LAUDERDALE
BROWARD COUNTY
THE EVERGLADES
DANIA
HOLLYWOOD
N. MIAMI BEACH
17
20
19
18
16
14
15
21
14- Barracuda Reef
15- Hammerhead Reef
16- Fisher's Pedestal
17- Lobster Ledge and Freighter Anchor
18- Old Houseboat and Barge
19- Mercedes
20- Rebel
21- Tenneco Towers
N

The wreck Mercedes *is a new addition to Ft. Lauderdale diving, and it is growing in popularity. This new site has added to the excitement associated with diving in Ft. Lauderdale.*

Typical depth range	:	30 feet
Typical current conditions	:	Light to moderate
Expertise required	:	None
Access	:	Boat or beach

Barracuda Reef is one of the more popular and frequently dived sites in the area. The reef site is south of the inlet at Port Everglades and is directly off the beach at the John U. Lloyd State Park in Dania.

The shallow corals of the middle reef come within 20 feet of the surface, making this site an excellent location for novice divers or snorkelers. The reef has a healthy concentration of staghorn, brain, and star corals, which are very common to the Florida Keys. The coral ledges on the inside of the reef rise more than 4 feet from the sand floor, creating coral tunnels that are a home to lobster and small spotted moray eels.

Because of the proximity of the reef to the beach, shore diving is quite popular here. For the first several dozen yards you will see mostly sand, and visibility tends to be poor because of the surf. Beyond the surf line the visibility improves and you begin to see the patchwork of the coral reef. Only good swimmers with proper floatation devices and a diver's flag should attempt this dive from the beach. There is a lot of boat traffic in the area and caution is advised.

In the shallow reef off Ft. Lauderdale, a diver swims side by side with a gray angelfish.

Star coral is found at Barracuda Reef. It is a spectacular macro-photography subject.

Typical depth range	:	50-80 feet
Typical current conditions	:	Variable to slight
Expertise required	:	Intermediate
Access	:	Boat

The deeper Hammerhead Reef lies directly seaward of Barracuda Reef in 50 to 80 feet of water. This coral system is the outer reef of the three reefs that run parallel to the beach. The coral ledges that rise more than 6 feet from the sand are pock-marked with crevices and deep undercuts. The top of the reef is overgrown with a large variety of lacy sea fans, and huge barrel and basket sponges. Along the face of the ledges, many small tropical fish can be observed among the soft oscillating corals.

There are wide sand channels that run between the long coral fingers at Hammerhead Reef. The winding paths provide breeding grounds for many species of conch, including the edible Queen conch. However, it is against Florida law to take Queen conch anywhere in state waters. Southern sting-rays are often found feeding in the area, and it is not uncommon to see large amberjacks, pompanos or an occasional nurse shark. This reef is very photogenic, and a good site to observe many of the ocean's larger schooling fish.

Night diving on this reef is exciting. This is a particularly good area for photography at night. The dark water creates a perfect contrast to the multi-colored coral polyps, purple sea anemones and small arrow crabs. Additionally, night diving allows the visiting diver the opportunity to observe parrotfish and sleeping squirrelfish up close. Do not startle the sleeping fish. They will panic and could swim blindly into the reefs.

A diver comforts a frightened puffer fish at Hammerhead Reef.

Coral ledges that make up Hammerhead Reef extend above the sand and are a niche for various marine life.

Typical depth range	:	30 feet
Typical current conditions	:	Variable
Expertise required	:	None
Access	:	Boat

Fisher's Pedestal is one of Ft. Lauderdale's more popular dive sites. This reef is located on the inside of the middle reef in a large open sand area. Three large coral pedestals resembling mushrooms protrude from the sand floor forming a triangle. One of the larger mounds has a long coral-encrusted overhang that is home to a large 4-foot barracuda.

This overhang is actually a cleaner station, and often large fish including the barracuda can be observed waiting their turn in line to be cleaned of parasites. Tiny blue gobies swim in and out of the gills and around the mouth of the barracuda in this strange symbiotic ecosystem.

The other mounds have large strands of staghorn corals that grow profusely around the crown. Beneath the coral crust, diffusely colored sponges grow in shades of blood red and neon green. Angelfish are often found flirting with each other as they playfully dart around the mounds. This is a good photographic site.

A sea whip flows in the gentle current at Fisher's Pedestal. It is best to check current conditions before you enter the water.

Among the different types of corals at Fisher's Pedestal, a large variety of sea life thrives. Pictured here is a yellow crinoid. Often barracuda are seen cruising ◄ the reefs.

Typical depth range	:	35 feet
Typical current conditions	:	Light
Expertise required	:	None
Access	:	Boat

Lobster Ledge is located south of the Howard Johnson's Hotel on Ft. Lauderdale Beach. This reef is very popular for underwater hunting. The shallow ledge is home to spiny lobster and hog snappers. Remember, hunt lobster only during the season, and don't take any shorts. Florida law is very strict and heavily enforced. Groupers are sometimes observed here. However, this area has been hunted regularly and it will take a diver's keen eye to come up with a catch.

Not far from this ledge, a large freighter anchor sits on a large barren sand plateau and serves as an excellent photo prop. The anchor weighs more than 10,000 lbs. and has a huge chain attached to the shank that runs north over the reef for more than 200 feet. The anchor has been down for several years, evident by the corals and sponge growth on its massive flukes.

Many of the local charter captains tend to overlook the anchor as a dive site because of its relatively small size for large dive groups. However, the anchor is an excellent photo location, and the resident family of Queen angelfish seem happy to serve as photographic subjects.

Near Lobster Ledge sits a large freighter anchor. This is another popular spot for photographers. The wrecked barge is now encrusted with red coral and sea fans. Photograph by Steven Lucas

A spiny lobster welcomes a visiting diver to its rocky environment at Lobster Ledge.

Typical depth range	:	70-80 feet
Typical current conditions	:	Moderate to strong
Expertise required	:	Intermediate
Access	:	Boat

One of the more interesting wrecks in the Ft. Lauderdale area is the old houseboat. Sunk over ten years ago to serve as an artificial reef, the wreck today is covered in soft corals and deep water gorgonians. A cloud of silver bait fish seems to cling to the side of the boat and part in perfect unison as a diver swims through. Just above the wreck, barracuda hang like lone sentinels guarding the houseboat.

Prior to its sinking, most of the furnishings were removed. Some of the kitchen cabinets and an old stove remain inside the intact structure. A diver could easily swim through the wreck from bow to stern.

The underwater photographer will find the houseboat wreck an especially exciting wreck for both wide-angle and close-up photography.

The barge wreck is a short swim from the houseboat. At over 100 feet long, the barge rests upright on the sand ocean floor 70 feet below the surface. It is covered in scarlet red coral and soft fuzzy sea fans. Deep water gorgonian sprout from the sides of the wreck, framing hatch openings that allow divers to swim through. Large sea turtles are sometimes found sleeping under the rounded bow.

A French angelfish heads for home on the barge and old houseboat wrecks.

The underwater photographer will find the houseboat and barge wrecks especially exciting for all type of photography.

Typical depth range	:	90-100 feet
Typical current conditions	:	Medium to strong
Expertise required	:	Intermediate to advanced
Access	:	Boat

The Mercedes is unquestionably the most famous of all the wrecks on Florida's east coast. Her notoriety started during a late November 1984 storm that thrashed monstrous waves against the Palm Beach coast. The high winds and strong waves broke the Mercedes from her safe mooring and drove the ship ashore. The huge ship was beached on the backyard of Palm Beach socialite, Mollie Wilmot, and quickly gained national attention.

The Mercedes sat abandoned for months as salvage crews furiously tried to drag the ship from the beach. The ship was soon declared a derelict, and the state of Florida was soon faced with the ominous task of removing

A diver explores the Mercedes wreck. Photograph by Steven Lucas

Sea life thrives around the ghostly image of the Mercedes.

it. After crews spent months trying to refloat the ship, the grip of the beach finally released its hold. The ship was then towed to Port Everglades at Ft. Lauderdale. Early in the spring of 1985, after it was cleaned and its doors and hatchways were removed, the ship was sunk to form an artificial reef and a playground for visiting divers.

Today, the 197-foot Mercedes rests upright and intact at 90 feet, her bow at 100 feet. A dive to this wreck includes some careful planning and a good knowledge of the dive tables. This wreck is one of the more popular dive sites, and as a result, it is usually quite easy to find, as many of the dive charters usually anchor above the wreck.

The superstructure remains intact, allowing divers to swim into the wheelhouse and around the decks. A large gaping hole near the bow, blown out by over 350 pounds of dynamite used to sink the ship, allows a view into the hold. All the doors and hatchways have been removed, making this a very safe dive. However, it is best to check the current conditions because sometimes the Gulf Stream will create strong surface conditions. With the currents, however, comes good visibility.

Typical depth range	:	110 feet
Typical current conditions	:	Medium to strong
Expertise required	:	Advanced
Access	:	Boat

One of the best wreck sites in the Ft. Lauderdale area is that of the 150-foot freighter, Rebel. Sunk in the summer of 1985, not more than 400 yards from the Mercedes, the Rebel sits upright and perfectly intact at 110 feet. The deck of the ship is at 85 feet, and when the clear waters of the Gulf Stream flow through, visibility exceeds 100 feet. This allows divers the opportunity to see the entire ship from just below the surface.

The ship sank adjacent to a low coral reef. Along the stern are low round mounds of coral emblazoned with red gorgonian. The wreck now has many large fish that cruise her decks, as well as schools of blue-striped grunts. The trick for having a good dive here is to properly secure the anchor downstream of the current. This will allow the diver to swim against the current while exploring the ship and return with ease upon ascent.

Preparing for a dive on the Rebel is essential. Divers should be well-equipped and have attained an advanced level of deep-water diving.

Serving as an artificial reef, the Rebel *is home to many fish. Here a diver looks into the engine room of the wreck.*

Visibility on the Rebel *wreck exceeds 100 feet. This diver sits in the wheelhouse of the wreck during a night dive.*

Typical depth range	:	60-120 feet
Typical current conditions	:	Medium
Expertise required	:	Intermediate
Access	:	Boat

The Tenneco Towers are a former Gulf of Mexico oil drilling platform that was donated, transported and sunk by the Tenneco Oil Company. Oil rigs have been proven as fish havens, and the new addition to the Ft. Lauderdale/Hollywood dive area is proving very effective as well. The oil rig was placed south of Hollywood near the Broward County line to allow dive operators in the Miami area the opportunity to enjoy this site.

The towers are made up of three major sections. Each was placed in depths of between 60 and 120 feet at 75- to 100-yard intervals. The shallowest one third is the upper derrick structure, the second third is the working deck, and the last third is the massive legs of the structure.

According to the Broward Dive Industry Association, this artificial reef is open to spearfishing; however, spearfishing on other reef and wreck sites is not permitted.

Caution is advised when diving the Tenneco Towers. There are large fish under the derrick and working deck of the structure. Make certain you have plenty of air when swimming under the platform. Remember, in an emergency situation, you will have to swim horizontally out from the structure before ascending.

Large fish often cruise the Tenneco Towers, where spearfishing is permitted.

Macro photographers will be quite busy at Tenneco Towers.

4

Diving in the Palm Beach Area

The Palm Beach coast offers some of the very best diving found anywhere in the state of Florida. All too often divers traveling through the state overlook the underwater opportunities here, for the more publicized diving in the Florida Keys. While each area of Florida offers its own unique aspect of diving, regular sightings of shark, turtles, dolphins and large jewfish are considered the forte of Palm Beach diving.

The waters around the Palm Beach area contain a number of sunken wrecks and barges that form artificial reefs. Some of the more recent wrecks that have been placed as marine preserves are the 120-foot freighter Eisaud and a 1967 Rolls Royce Silver Shadow.

Drift Diving. The Gulf Stream is closest to the coast at this point, and most of the diving is usually deep with very strong currents. However, the Palm Beach dive operators have their own very simple diving technique called "drift diving," which is very simple and safe.

Drift diving is the most popular form of diving in the Palm Beach area. Usually, the dive guide will handle the tag line which consists of a long nylon rope of 100 feet or more. Attached to the one end is a large orange floating ball; the other end is held by the dive guide while underwater. The group of divers simply descend to the ocean floor and allow the current to gently glide them across the coral terrain. On the surface the orange ball keeps track of the divers, and the charter boat captain simply follows. Upon surfacing, the boat is nearby and easily boarded. Drift diving the Palm Beach area is one of the easiest and most relaxing forms of covering great distances underwater.

Turtle Watching. During the warm evenings of the early summer, usually between the months of May and July, a remarkable phenomenon occurs. Female sea turtles, loggerheads, green turtles and leatherback turtles leave the safety of the ocean and crawl towards the cool sand of the darkened beaches.

The huge turtles, after finding a convenient location on the beach, begin to scoop, with their back flippers, holes large and deep enough to deposit hundreds of small eggs.

During the months of the late summer and early fall, the small hatchlings begin to crawl from their sand-covered eggs towards the ocean. The small sea turtles then begin a long maturation process, and like clockwork, repeat the life cycle every year.

The sea turtles are an endangered species, and there is probably no greater concern for their continued existence than in the Palm Beach area.

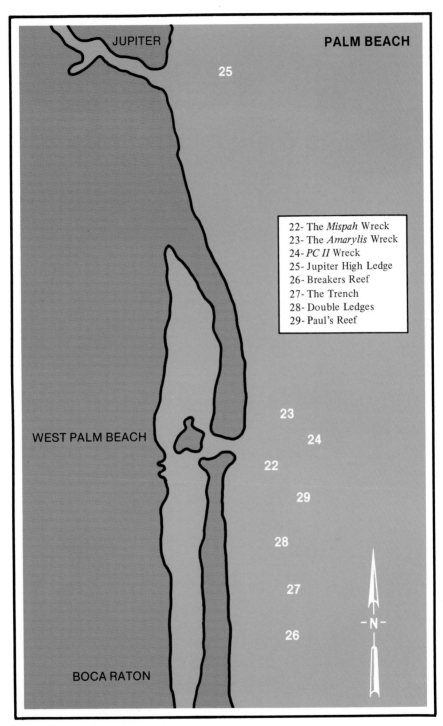

JUPITER

PALM BEACH

25

22- The *Mispah* Wreck
23- The *Amarylis* Wreck
24- *PC II* Wreck
25- Jupiter High Ledge
26- Breakers Reef
27- The Trench
28- Double Ledges
29- Paul's Reef

23

24

WEST PALM BEACH

22

29

28

27

-N-

26

BOCA RATON

Each dive site off Palm Beach offers its own variety of excitement. In many areas, turtles, dolphins and sharks can be seen interacting amid the colorful flora of the Palm Beach reefs.

In areas off Palm Beach, endangered turtles are now protected by law. Do not harass or disturb them, especially while they are nesting. Photograph by Steven Lucas

When diving in this area, it is almost guaranteed that you will see one of these large prehistoric-looking beasts. It is illegal to harass or ride the turtles; however, the opportunity to swim next to these graceful creatures and photograph them is truly unique to Palm Beach.

Sea turtles are fascinating animals uniquely designed to live in the ocean. Every time a turtle dies, there is a greater chance for the extinction of one of the ocean's most interesting inhabitants. Never harass or disturb nesting turtles or small hatchlings. Be careful to avoid collisions with turtles while boating. They are air-breathers and come up to the surface to breath. Do not throw trash or plastic bags into the ocean. The sea turtle's main diet is jellyfish, and often plastic bags are mistaken for food. Sea turtles cannot digest the plastic, and they will most likely die.

Conch is fairly popular in areas of Palm Beach. This area is also well-known for its fantastic wreck diving.

Typical depth range	:	90 feet
Typical current conditions	:	Medium to strong
Expertise required	:	Intermediate to advanced
Access	:	Boat

The wreck of the Greek luxury liner Mispah is one of the more popular wreck sites that attract divers to the Palm Beach area. Lying almost intact in 90 feet of water, the 185-foot vessel is only a short boat ride from the Palm Beach inlet. The Mispah was purposely sunk more than 16 years ago to form an artificial reef and a new legally protected fish preserve where spear-fishing and collecting of marine tropicals is prohibited.

A school of spade fish patrol the reefs around the 185-foot wreck, the Mispah.

The Mispah *was one of the many ships sunk to create artificial reefs in the Palm Beach area. The Artificial Reef Program has greatly enhanced the marine population of Florida's east coast.*

Today, the Mispah sits nearly intact, but it is showing signs of deterioration. Local dive operators recommend not penetrating the cabins and main salon areas. Some of the wreck has collapsed, and there is always the possibility of being seriously hurt inside the wreck. However, exploring the exterior of the wreck can make for a safe and fun-filled dive. Swimming around the multi-tiered decks and down the exterior passageways is very exciting.

The Mispah is an underwater photographer's dream. The wreck is alive with macro-marine creatures that cover the vessel's structure from bow to stern. The cargo holds that once contained food supplies and passenger luggage are now home to thousands of schooling reef fish. The bow of the luxury liner is now torn open by years of battering storm activity. A large chunk of metal lies to her port bow. Schooling grunts, mahogany snappers and Bermuda chub shroud her gashed bow and flow in perfect unison in the clear Gulf Stream waters.

Typical depth range	:	90-100 feet
Typical current conditions	:	Medium to strong
Expertise required	:	Intermediate to advanced
Access	:	Boat

One of the wrecks that has been a favorite attraction for many years is the sunken freighter Amarylis. The Amarylis was an island freighter that was sunk by local authorities to create an artificial reef and boost the charter fishing business. The 300-foot vessel sits upright in less than 100 feet of water, a short swim from the Mispah wreck. When the conditions are right, many of the professional dive charter captains will plan a drift dive over both wrecks.

The superstructure of the ship was removed prior to sinking, and most of the decking was removed or has since collapsed. Visibility often exceeds 100 feet on the wreck, and when this occurs the ship looks like a giant open john-boat from just under the surface.

The diving conditions found here are typical of the Palm Beach area. Swimming through the hull of the wreck is the easiest and safest way of exploring the ship. The structure will offer protection from the strong Gulf Stream current.

Hundreds of schooling fish patrol the Amarylis *wreck off Palm Beach.* ➤

Typical depth range	:	100 feet
Typical current conditions	:	Variable, strong
Expertise required	:	Advanced
Access	:	Boat

The PC II wreck was a military patrol craft that now rests in 100 feet of water. The vessel has been broken in half and the stern section looks much like an old barge. The wreck is not far from the Palm Beach inlet that forms the main channel to the intracoastal waterway.

The PC II is an interesting dive, but because of the varying current conditions and the depth involved, this dive is usually reserved for more advanced divers.

The Gulf Stream is less than one mile from the Palm Beach shore and at tidal changes the current can exceed three knots. It is wise to dive at slack tide periods; however, a secure anchor line, a trailing safety line of at least 100 feet and a current line that runs from the point of entry into the water from your boat to the anchor line will make this a safer dive. Once on the wreck, remaining on the leeward side of the current should make for an exciting, safe dive.

As a result of the proximity of the Gulf Stream, large oceanic denizens are often sighted in the area. The PC II is a good wreck for the underwater hunter. Each dive promises the excitement of discovery.

A photogenic gray angelfish poses for the camera near the PC II *wreck.*

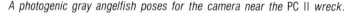

A diver examines areas of the sunken military patrol craft, the PC II. The wreck lies in 100 feet of water off Palm Beach.

Typical depth range	:	40-90 feet
Typical current conditions	:	Variable, strong
Expertise required	:	Intermediate
Access	:	Boat

The town of Jupiter is north of Palm Beach and marked by a tall stone lighthouse. Offshore, the Gulf Stream flows parallel to the beach. Less than one mile from the shoreline the continental shelf drops into the deep Atlantic Ocean. All along the coral face, long narrow fissures are etched into the rock ledges by the constant currents. One of those ledges is the popular Jupiter High Ledge.

The ledge is several miles in length, and in areas it jumps from the sand ocean floor at 90 feet, up to a depth of 65 feet. The face of the ledge is deeply pock-marked with crevasses and small caves. Large grouper and lobster are often found here, as well as several friendly green moray eels. The large moray eels are used to being fed by visiting divers and often they will leave their rocky homes for a small food handout.

The reef system at Jupiter is an excellent location for underwater photography, and the reef creatures are usually quite cooperative. This area is one of those places where you never know what might appear from out of the deep blue ocean. Large horse-eyed jacks often cruise the reef, and turtles can be found sleeping under many of the small ledges. As a result of the abundance of marine life, and the expanse of the coral ledge, drift diving is usually done on this dive.

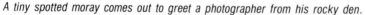

A tiny spotted moray comes out to greet a photographer from his rocky den.

A group of divers hand-feed a large, gentle green moray that lives among the rocks at Jupiter High Ledge. Photograph by Steven Lucas

Typical depth range	:	60-80 feet
Typical current conditions	:	Variable, medium
Expertise required	:	Novice
Access	:	Boat

The Breakers Reef is easily located offshore by lining your boat directly east of the Breakers Hotel in Palm Beach. The reef line runs north and south, parallel to the shoreline. The inside of the reef is in 60 feet of water, and the outer ledge is in the 80-foot range.

A diver searches for signs of marine life near a coral head. Coral grows thickly and provides a home to many fish species at Breakers Reef.

The corals usually grow in abundance in the medium depth ranges. Here, though, there seem to be more barren areas and the limestone rocks show the results of heavy diving activity. Of course, with the Gulf Stream so close, the real excitement is the unexpected. Divers have encountered large grouper, moray eels, schools of dog snapper and an occasional nurse shark.

However, throughout the world large animals such as amberjack, pompano, and sharks are found in areas where food if prolific. These feeding sites are often reefs and ledges that are constantly cleansed with nutrient-rich waters that support the varied marine life.

The presence of sharks is not a reason for concern. The sound of a group of divers and their trailing bubbles is enough to send any large predator on its way.

Although Breakers Reef is more known for its large fish, such as grouper, sharks and dog snapper, divers often encounter hidden beauties like this large horse conch. Photograph by Steven Lucas

Typical depth range	:	60 feet
Typical current conditions	:	None to slight
Expertise required	:	Novice
Access	:	Boat

The Trench is man-made, created over 15 years ago to lay the Boca Raton sewage outfall pipe. The very sharp and prominent cut has quickly become overgrown with hard corals and brilliant-hued soft sponges. The walls of the Trench are lined with schooling porkfish and grunts, and spadefish are often found cruising the upper ledges. Small spotted yellow rays that measure up to 15 inches can be found buried beneath the sand floor. Though the small rays look totally harmless, they can inflict serious pain if stepped on or carelessly handled.

The Trench is easily located offshore of the Boca Raton Beach Pavillion. Near the shoreline in 60 feet of water, it runs east and west, and perpendicular to the current. At the seaward end of the Trench the water is more than 90 feet deep and trails off into the Gulf Stream. The Trench intersects all three reef systems, and starting at the inside ledge, the 20-foot-wide corridor's cliffs rise more than 15 feet from the sand floor.

As a result of the high cliffs, divers are able to swim the entire length of the Trench relatively easily as the currents flow overhead.

Green morays seem to consider themselves very photogenic. They'll gladly pose for the underwater photographer.

To the south of the Trench is a very interesting series of vertical ledges that run north and south along the inside reef. The ledges rise 8 to 12 feet from the sand ocean floor and are pitted with numerous holes that provide perfect nesting for the Florida spiny lobster. To the west of these ledges is another reef ridge that rises 4 to 6 feet from the sand floor. This reef is covered in hard corals and is home to tiny tropical fish.

Color abounds in fairly shallow water. Here a diver glances up at a species of soft coral.

Typical depth range	:	70-90 feet
Typical current conditions	:	Variable to strong
Expertise required	:	Intermediate
Access	:	Boat

The Double Ledges has been one of the more popular reef sites visited by local Palm Beach divers for many years. The ledges resemble the tiered steps of some giant staircase leading into the unknown depths of the ocean. The shallower ledge is in the 70-foot range and rises vertically over 6 feet from the sand floor. The second ledge is much deeper and a short distance swim further west. The barren sand plateau between the ledges gently slopes to the crest of the second dropoff. This ledge is a sheer drop over 8 feet to the

Besides numerous lobster and crabs, Double Ledges has been known for its colorful fish population.

Christmas tree worms, though small, add lively splashes of color to the dropoffs at Double Ledges.

sand floor to a depth of 90 feet. From this point the sloping bottom gently rolls off into the Atlantic Ocean.

The 20 minutes alotted for this depth is enough time to get a good overview of the ledges. Lobster and stone crabs can be taken from these reefs during the legal season. However, remember to measure the lobster. From the base of its outer shell to the crown of its head between the horns must be a minimum of 3 inches. Stone crabs are also very edible and delightfully delicious. However, these crabs may only be taken during the legal season.

The stone crab season runs between October 15 and May 15. To be legal, a stone crab must have a forearm at least 2-3/4 inches long. Only remove one claw and release the crab. Leaving one claw will allow the crab to defend itself while the other, missing claw rejuvenates.

It is always best to check with local authorities prior to removing any marine life from the ocean. Many dive operators have their own policies about protecting their reefs.

Typical depth range	:	50-60 feet
Typical current conditions	:	Variable to mild
Expertise required	:	Novice
Access	:	Boat

Paul's Reef is farther south near the town of Lake Worth. This reef is a good site for the novice or intermediate diver. The depth range is 50 feet, and little or no current seems to be normal for this site.

The reef is typical of the ridge systems found in the Palm Beach area. The ridge runs along the shoreline on the inside of the middle reef. The ledge rises more than 5 feet from the sand, and is covered in sea fans and abounds in small tropical fish.

This area is an excellent night diving reef—small creatures expand their oscillating plumes into the rich waters, while small nudibranchs cover the hard corals in their search for food. An occasional octopus can be found tucked away in some little nook in the side of the cliff, and large parrotfish can be observed up close in their protective webs as they sleep.

When the water is calm, visibility can exceed 100 feet and this area can be reached by swimming from the beach. However, currents have to be observed, and careful dive planning is necessary.

Parrotfish change color at different stages of growth. Here at Paul's Reef, a large group swims together, feeding on the coral.

Many divers enjoy interacting with a puffer fish. These fish puff themselves up for protection from predators.

5

Safety

This section discusses common hazards, including dangerous marine animals, and emergency procedures in case of a diving accident. Included are some very useful phone numbers and addresses of authorities and emergency contacts. The diagnosis and treatment of serious medical problems are not discussed here. Refer to your first aid manual or emergency diving accident manual for that information.

A group of divers gather prior to surfacing. Always plan your dive and dive your plan.

This scorpionfish remains well camouflaged, even though the waters surrounding the Amarylis wreck are extremely clear.

Wreck Diving. Diving a wreck can be fun, and if certain basic precautions are followed before entering a wreck, it can also be safe. Wreck diving is a specialty and requires advanced training. All divers should keep in mind that they should never penetrate a wreck unless properly trained. Entering a wreck is similar to cave diving and the same precautions should be observed. Some basic precautions are:

• Do not enter a wreck without at least two reliable underwater lights per diver.
• Avoid tight entrances.
• Move slowly to avoid clouding visibility with silt.
• Attach a line to the outside of the wreck.
• Before entering any part of a wreck, examine the space carefully for objects hanging from the ceiling and other potential hazards.

Emergency Services

Divers Alert Network (DAN)
(919) 684-8111

United States Coast Guard
7000 N. Ocean Dr.
Dania, FL
(305) 927-1611

52 SW 1 Ave.
Miami, FL
(305) 536-5611

Dive-Med International
3001 S. Hanover St.
Baltimore, MD 21225
(Contact for a list of physicians in area who specialize in dive medicine.)

Florida Underwater Council
P.O. Box 431407
Miami, FL 33143

Florida Marine Patrol
Ft. Lauderdale, FL
(305) 467-4541

Miami, FL
(305) 325-3346

West Palm Beach, FL
(305) 747-2033

Manatee Injury Report
1-800-342-1821

Recompression Chambers

South Miami Hospital
7400 SW 62nd Ave.
Miami, FL 33143
(305) 661-4611

Photographers find extraordinary subjects in all areas of Florida's eastern coastline.

Feeding moray eels can be dangerous even though many people do it. If you insist on giving food to these creatures (who by the way are quite capable of acquiring their own), wear gloves and be cautious. However, it is best to leave them alone. *Photograph by Steven Lucas*

NOAA-Florida Underwater Council
75 Virginia Beach Dr.
Virginia Key, Miami, FL 33149
(305) 596-8576

Intercity First Aid Squad
640 Old Dixie Hwy.
West Palm Beach, FL 33403
(305) 844-6577

Dangerous Marine Animals

Sharks. The most common shark found in the waters of Florida's east coast is the nurse shark. Bull sharks and black-tipped sharks are also common but rarely seen. The nurse shark is usually found sleeping under a ledge and though it is usually docile, it has been known to be aggressive when harassed. When any shark begins to get too close it is best to leave the water.

Jellyfish, Hydroids, Man-O-War. Jellyfish are not aggressive creatures. They will usually be floating on or near the surface flowing with the current. They pose more of a hazard for the snorkeler than the diver; however, it is best upon surfacing to look up and avoid contact with the jellyfish.

Eels. There are several species of eels: green moray, spotted moray, goldentail, viper and purplemouth moray. All the species live in caves or under ledges, and while not typically aggressive, they can inflict a serious wound when harassed. Try to avoid all contact with the eels.

Sting Rays. Sting rays are often found in the sandy flats between the reef ridges or near the wrecks. Rays are beautiful creatures and are for the most part harmless, but many have a large barb on the end of their tails, and this barb could inflict serious pain if contacted.

Scorpionfish. Scorpionfish are very common on the wrecks and reefs of South Florida. They are less than a foot long and are very well camouflaged. They look similar to a coral-covered rock and can inflict great pain if touched. Usually, an unsuspecting diver kneels or sits on one of these ugly creatures. Watch for the long poisonous spines hidden along its fins.

Barracuda. Barracuda are usually everywhere you look. Typically, the "cuda" will hang on the outer fringes of visibility. It is usually considered more curious than ferocious. If you are harassed by a menacing barracuda it is best to leave the area or to get out of the water.

Appendix

Dive Stores and Charters

PALM BEACH

American Divers International
409 Lake Ave.
Lake Worth, FL 33460
(305) 582-0877

Aquashop Diving Center
1940 Broadway
Riviera Beach, FL 33404
(305) 848-)9042

Coastal Sport and Dive Shop
2407 10th Ave.
Lake Worth, FL 33460
(305) 965-0524

Dive Masters of Jupiter Inc.
18487 US 1
Tequesta, FL 33458
(305) 744-6111

Divers Express Inc.
3516 Collin Dr.
West Palm Beach, FL 33406
(305) 439-0519

Dive Shop II
700 Casa Lorna Blvd.
Boynton Beach, FL 33435
(305) 278-9111

Force E
877 E. Palmetto Park Rd.
Boca Raton, FL 33432
(305) 368-0555

Force E
1399 N. Military Trail
West Palm Beach, FL 33409
(305) 471-2676

Frank's Dive Shop
301 E. Blue Heron Blvd.
Riviera Beach, FL 33404
(305) 848-7632

Gold Coast Charters
113 Timber Run East
West Palm Beach, FL 33407
(305) 842-6356

Gulf Stream Diver Scuba Charters
2315 Caroma Lane
West Palm Beach, FL 33406
(305) 965-7878

Joalexa Charters
1891 Juno Isles Blvd.
Juno, FL 33408
(305) 622-7543

Jupiter-Tequesta Scuba Sports
150 US 1
Tequesta, FL 33458
(305) 746-1555

Kollers Reef Scuba Charter
413 11408 83rd Lane
Lake Park, FL 33410
(305) 626-5537

Loxahatchee Dive Shop
304 Old Dixie Hwy.
Jupiter, FL 33458
(305) 747-6115

Norine Rouse Scuba Club
4708 N. Dixie Hwy.
West Palm Beach, FL 33407
(305) 844-2466

Ocean Exposures
1165 E. Blue Heron Blvd.
Riviera Beach, FL 33404
(305) 848-9135

Ocean Quest Charter Inc.
21261 Hazelwood Lane
Boca Raton, FL 33428
(305) 487-1373

Reef Dive Shop
304 E. Ocean Ave.
Lantan, FL 33462
(305) 585-1425

Seapro Scuba Center
3619 Broadway
Riviera Beach, FL 33404
(305) 844-3483

Subsea Aquatics Inc.
17967 US 1
Jupiter, FL 33468
(305) 744-6674

World of Scuba
902 S. Federal Hwy.
Lantana, FL 33460
(305) 586-3164

FT. LAUDERDALE

Adventure Divers
922 SE 20th Street
Ft. Lauderdale, FL 33316
(305) 523-8354

Brent Feinmans Scuba World
3932 Davie Blvd.
Ft. Lauderdale, FL
(305) 587-7234

Brooks Family Undersea Sports
1525 N. Federal Hwy.
Ft. Lauderdale, FL
(305) 564-8661

Divers Den
8280 State Road 84
Davie, FL
(305) 473-9455

Divers Haven
1530 SE Cordova Rd.
Ft. Lauderdale, FL
(305) 524-2112

Divers Unlimited
6023 Hollywood Blvd.
Hollywood, FL
(305) 981-0156

Expeditions Unlimited
2632 NE 4th St.
Pompano Beach, FL
(305) 946-9187

Ft. Lauderdale Divers
940 NE 20th Ave.
Ft. Lauderdale, FL
(305) 522-7722

Int'l. Scuba Academy
15 N. Federal Hwy.
Pompano, FL
(305) 782-5768

Lauderdale Diver
1334 SE 17th St.
Ft. Lauderdale, FL
(305) 467-2822

Pro Dive Shop
Bahia Mar Yachting Center
Ft. Lauderdale, FL
(305) 761-3413

Pro Dive
2507 N. Ocean Blvd.
Pompano Beach, FL 33062
(305) 942-3000

Scuba-Rific
4282 S. University Dr.
Davie, FL
(305) 473-6833

Scuba Sports Inc.
1802 N. University Dr.
Plantation, FL
(305) 474-2555

Scuba II
5060 N. Dixie Hwy.
Oakland Park, FL
(305) 772-3483

Submariner
940 NE 20th Ave.
Ft. Lauderdale, FL
(305) 522-7722

Sportsmens Paradise
2800 N. Federal Hwy.
Ft. Lauderdale, FL
(305) 563-1900

Weatherproof Systems Inc.
3569 N. Dixie Hwy.
Oakland Park, FL
(305) 565-1771

MIAMI

AAA Scuba School
Homestead, FL
(305) 247-4198

American Sport Diving Schools
18578 SW 89th Pl.
Miami, FL
(305) 253-5353

Anything Underwater
6887 SW 40th St.
Miami, FL
(305) 662-1118

Aquatic Divers Inc.
1206 Stirling Rd.
Dania, FL
(305) 925-8119

Aquanauts Dive Shop
677 SW 1st St.
Miami, FL
(305) 545-9000

Aquanauts Dive Shop
903 SW 87th Ave.
Miami, FL
(305) 262-9295

Around The World Sports Center
9849 Bird Rd.
Miami, FL
(305) 221-7182

Austing Diving Center
10503 S. Dixie Hwy.
Miami, FL
(305) 665-0636

Biscayne Aqua Center
Biscayne National Park
Homestead, FL
(305) 247-2400

Boulevard Dive Shop
7111 Biscayne Blvd.
Miami, FL
(305) 758-1600

Boulevard Sports Center
16150 Biscayne Blvd.
North Miami Beach, FL
(305) 945-6111

Caribbean Island Divers
8347 Bird Rd.
Miami, FL
(305) 551-7300

Cutler Ridge Diving Center
20850 S. Dixie Hwy.
Miami, FL
(305) 251-2710

Divers Den South
12614 N. Kendall Dr.
Miami, FL
(305) 595-2010

Divers Dream Inc.
903 SW 87th Ave.
Miami, FL
(305) 262-9295

Divers Paradise Corp.
13854 SW 56th St.
Miami, FL
(305) 387-9100

The Diving Locker
223 Sunny Isles Blvd.
North Miami Beach, FL
(305) 947-6025

El Capitan Sports Center
1590 NW 27th Ave.
Miami, FL
(305) 635-7500

Genesis Diving & Watersports
18555 S. Dixie Hwy.
Miami, FL
(305) 255-3483

Happy Divers
767 NE 79th St.
Miami, FL
(305) 754-2296

Key Divers Inc.
200 Crandon Blvd.
Key Biscayne, FL
(305) 361-1993

Native Diver Charter Service
1438 NE 105th St.
North Miami Shores, FL
(305) 895-2538

New England Divers Inc.
6043 NW 167th St.
Miami, FL
(305) 825-7722

OceanQuest Dive Shop Inc.
6500 W. 4th Ave.
Hialeah, FL
(305) 556-9866

Pisces Divers Inc.
1290 5th St.
Miami Beach, FL
(305) 534-7710

RJ Diving Ventures Inc.
15560 NE 5th Ave.
Miami, FL
(305) 940-1182

Scorpio Enterprises Co. Inc.
677 SW 1st St.
Miami, FL
(305) 545-9000

Scuba Sports Inc.
6604 SW 57th Ave.
South Miami, FL
(305) 662-2568

Tarpoon Skin Diving Center
3200 Palm Ave.
Hialeah, FL
(305) 887-8726

Underwater Unlimited
4633 Le Jeune Rd.
Coral Gables, FL
(305) 445-7837

Index